Capitalism

is the Problem

Ron Jacobs

ISBN: 978-1-944388-14-0

Fomite
Burlingon, VT
http://www.fomitepress.com

The United States is in crisis. The world is in crisis. It is a crisis that impoverishes millions more every year while enhancing the wealth of the rarefied few who conspire with politicians to make it so. It is a crisis that manifests itself in endless and meaningless wars. It is a crisis that dismantles schools, hospitals, roads, and other infrastructure in the name of private profit. Most ominously, it is a crisis which diminishes the health of the earth's ecosystem, undoing an already fragile environment in order to squeeze dollars from that which gives all earthly species life.

This truth is grounded in the fact of the super-exploitation that occurs in the nations that make up the "developing" world -- a world located primarily in the southern hemisphere, but also exists in primarily non-white regions of the northern hemisphere as well; in sweatshops and the euphemistically labeled Enterprise Zones of China, Mexico and other large manufacturing nations. Complementary to the new imperialism, and almost as fundamental, is how international loan and aid agencies like the World Bank and the International Monetary Fund (IMF) utilize economic theories beneficial to their strategy of keeping wealth in the banks of the northern capitalist nations Because of their strategy of outsourcing the profits from this production go overwhelmingly into the financial houses of the super-capitalist nations in the north, mostly to those in the United States and a couple of nations in Europe.

Capitalism is based on the exploitation of labor. It always has been and always will be. In today's world of global capitalism, where low-cost goods are made by low-paid workers around the world, that exploitation has become what is known as super-exploitation. As John Smith wrote in his 2015 exploration of modern day imperialism:

> "So long as workers are obliged to work for longer than the labor-time needed to produce their basket of consumption goods, they are exploited. This is independent of the specific way their labor is employed and of whether they are employed in production, circulation, or administration. (63, *Twenty-first Century Imperialism*)."

Another form this exploitation takes seems almost feudal at times, and can best be labeled debt peonage. Because virtually nobody who sells their labor to make a living actually gets paid enough to afford that living, they must borrow money. Perhaps one borrows money to buy a car or a house; perhaps they go into debt for leisure goods like a TV or iPod; or perhaps their debt is related to getting a college degree. No matter the reason, the final result is that they owe someone or something money. That something is usually a bank or other financial institution. Besides the actual amount borrowed, the lender will also charge interest on the loan. Often, (especially in the case of consumer credit like credit cards) the interest is usurious. This means that there is virtually no way for the debtor to ever pay off their loan, since most of their payments are going to pay the interest. In the case of loans for higher education, there is the added fact that the debtor is required by law to pay such loans and can never renege on them by declaring bankruptcy. So, instead of just being taken advantage of by one's employer, working people are also at the mercy of those to whom they owe money for the things they need or desire to live a decent life.

The only genuine anti-capitalist struggle is one with the goal of destroying existing class relationships. Such a struggle cannot be waged by separating workplace issues from those of the community; in other words, one cannot separate rent, mortgages, privatization of public space from that which makes living both communally and privately better.

In order to understand the actual nature of the working class under capitalism, we should view the world of working people as an organic whole. This means that housing, utility access and costs are workplace issues; childcare and education too. Affordable housing and food costs are more than secondary concerns. Their role in taking back wages provides another means for the capitalist system to maintain its control. Debt, whether incurred via consumer, housing, education or vehicle loans in the advanced capitalist world or incurred via a micro-loan program in the developing nations, is still debt peonage. The increasing cost of post-secondary education throughout the world and the mortgage crisis are both tools of neoliberal capitalism that ensure the continued upward motion of capital.

In the mid-1980s I lived and worked in a small town on the Olympic Peninsula in Washington State. The town had been founded by logging interests in the early part of the twentieth century and, after some battles between industry and workers, had thrived for several decades prior to the 1980s. Workers made good wages for hard work, the corporation made big profits and the town had a decent school, a fair housing stock, and supported a robust small-town economy. By 1985, this small town scenario had changed drastically. The recession that began in 1973 and was exacerbated by the advent of neoliberal capitalism and the austerity politics of Jimmy Carter and Ronald Reagan ravaged that town. Most of the harvested timber was being towed offshore to a non-union mill that cut the logs into boards. Meanwhile, the mill in town had gone from three plants running three shifts down to one plant and running two shifts that made pressed wood products. Over half of the mill workers had lost their jobs while the loggers—who were mostly independents—saw their prices drop and their stock decrease as clear-cutting took over the industry.

When I arrived, the only jobs in town were in the tourist industry (fishing, hunting and hiking), food service, the illicit marijuana cultivation trade, and one small plant on the edge of town getting outsourced work from the new computer industry taking over the suburbs west of Seattle under the aegis of Bill Gates and Microsoft. This is where I got a job. The pay was abysmal at $2.85 an hour, the work was tedious, and the layoffs came about every three months. When there was work, we would often work sixty hours a week. Most of my co-workers were the wives of mill workers permanently laid off, taking the jobs to supplement their laid-off partner's unemployment benefits. During the weeks I was laid off from the electronics plant, some friends paid me to take care of their marijuana plants. The only thing certain about the job security at the plant was its uncertainty. No matter what, though, the rent was still due and the kid had to be fed. So I did what I had to. My situation was not unusual. Indeed, it is even more the norm for low-income workers now than it was in the early years of neoliberalism when I experienced it.

I mention this part of my biography to make a point about what I consider very important human elements of contemporary imperialism. The first concerns what is euphemistically termed flexibility in employment. This term is used to define several modern forms of labor, including but not limited to, subcontracting work like that of Uber drivers, temporary and/or part-time employment either directly through a firm or through an agency, and the cycle of work-then-layoff-then-work I describe above. The intent and purpose of this type of "flexible" employment is to remove the negative effects of the increasingly volatile financial market from the industry, and force the workers to bear the brunt of its ups and downs (mostly downs.) This manipulation of labor has given the employers more leeway in hiring by creating a surplus labor population that is global in nature, while also ensuring that market downturns are less likely to destroy the employers' capital. The fate of those without little or no capital is none of the employers' concern.

This is one reason why people voted for Trump. Although voting for Trump as a protest made some kind of sense, the reality is that voting for Trump was anything but a protest. It was instead a vote for the most reactionary elites of US capitalism. The fact that it was considered a protest is the clearest proof that the electoral system in place in the United States is a restrictive system on par with the few one party states that bother to hold elections. The 2016 choices of both major parties represented the most reactionary of the ruling capitalist elites. Once the party nominations were in, there was no choice that might represent working people of all identities. Of course, there is a larger argument that under any system of monopoly capitalism, democracy based on the principle of one person one vote is impossible. In the United States, the judicial decision equating corporations to persons further eliminates any possibility of all votes being equal.

Capitalism will continue to boom and bust (probably ever more frequently) with the lowest paid workers bearing the brunt of this cycle. The stopgap measures that have kept capitalism going are ultimately unsustainable. This is why we see crashes and peaks happening more frequently; it is also why we see more people living in shelters, and on the streets. It is why wars seem never to end and the ecological situation only worsens. It is the latter that will most likely kill us all. Cuban revolutionary leader Raúl Valdés Vivó, wrote "(this) is "un crisis sin salida del capitalismo," a crisis with no capitalist way out. The only way forward for humanity is to "begin the transition to a communist mode of production. . . . Either the people will destroy the imperialist power and establish their own, or the end of history. It is not 'socialism or barbarism,' as Rosa Luxemburg said in 1918, but socialism or nothing."

Speaking of Rosa Luxemburg, it was she who predicted the current situation a century ago. In essence, she told her readers that more money than ever would be made in this stage of capitalism, but, more than ever it would be made by a smaller number of people. Furthermore, those who will make the money produce nothing but debt and war. The ravages of capitalism are shared by all except the wealthy to varying degrees. In what is now perfectly clear, when the profits of the latter are threatened everyone else pays. Health care becomes scarcer, as do good paying jobs; education is stripped to its barest essentials or privatized; police and prison budgets are expanded and the victims of these ravages are blamed for these attacks on their being.

In short, capitalism is a con game and a swindle. This is a greater truth now than ever because the system of capitalism is running out of tricks to keep itself alive. The version called neoliberalism is little more than the latest swindle, and seems to be one with a rather short life. Donald Trump's answer to go backwards in economic history, pretending that the US economy can return to one of its heydays. He has promised his proletarian voters that he will bring back good paying production jobs like the ones that existed in the so-called rust belt until the 1970s. The likelihood is that the best he'll be able to do is bring back a version of an earlier heyday—the time of the robber barons. The workers will get some industrial jobs back, but they won't be getting paid very much for doing them.

It's quite likely Donald Trump knows this, but tells his supporters otherwise. His rich supporters and friends definitely know it. There's a reason why the trading floor of the New York Stock Exchange has been in a frenzy since Trump's election. They know that their time to take advantage of the swindle is now. Speculators can lie and cheat at will, taking the money they never worked for and turning it into that many more empty dollars. Like Trump and his investments, the traders understand that they can make money without any evidence their buyers will, and if the investment fails they will get bailed out. Trump got rich in part by repeatedly enacting this scenario. The big financial houses and banks performed similar feats that ended with being bailed out by

US taxpayers after the crash of 2007-2008. They know another bailout is available for the next time they crash the market.

So, what does this have to do with Donald Trump and his government? Most obvious is the fact that the United States is a capitalist and imperialist nation, its economic situation both dependent on the rest of the world's economies, and essential to their continued existence. The last thirty or so years have seen this interconnectedness increase in large part because US-based multinational corporations have moved their operations overseas in search of cheap labor. The other aspect of this transition is the billions of dollars from foreign interests which have been invested in property and businesses in the United States. Donald Trump is part and parcel of this mechanism. Like his right wing supporters' enemy George Soros, his billions come from the manipulation of monies and speculation. His claim that he will bring industry back to the US and give working people good paying jobs cannot work in this reality. His statements in this regard are either outright lies, or display ignorance of how monopoly capitalism actually works. His financial holdings suggest it is the former. In other words, he knows he is telling his working class voters a lie.

The reason he gets away with this (and all the other lies he manages to get away with) is because—as numerous studies have shown—the media shares the ideology he represents. Since the advent of FOX News, the influence of the most right wing, proto-fascist elements of the ruling elites has increased. It no longer matters if the truth is told. Furthermore, more and more residents don't seem to care about truth either. Perhaps better than any other political figure on the national stage, Donald Trump understands this. Indeed, he replicates this lack of concern and turns it into a principle, creating a base of support which is both angry and authoritarian. The potential for violence simmers constantly under the surface, revealing itself so far only randomly. It also justifies the violence of the State when it is turned against their common enemies.

I would like to emphasize what I noted before—that capitalism seems to be running out of tricks to keep itself alive. Despite instances of what seem to be proof the opposite is true: neoliberalism's constant privatization, Trumpism's retreat to economic nationalism, government bailout of corporations and banks; I would argue that these are last-ditch efforts that will only delay its final scene upon the world stage. Of course, if the scale of ecological destruction continues at its current pace (or intensifies, which is quite possible), that final scene will not only spell the end of capitalism; it will also spell the end of the world as we know it. This is why capitalism itself must end.

Resistance Must be Radical in its Understanding of the Problem

The opposition to Trump and the right wing government he heads needs to be radical. It should not just be a personalized campaign against Trump and Pence. It cannot merely lead us back to the Democratic Party of Obama and Clinton, whose segment of the political class is part of the problem. Their primary difference with Trump seems to be around how much racism and misogyny will be tolerated, at least in terms of their public face. Democrats are more inclusive of non-white-males with money than the GOP. This does not mean that, when put into practice, many of their policies are any less racist and misogynist than those preferred by the GOP. It does mean that Nazis and Klansmen prefer the Republican Party because of the very public and very obvious racism and misogyny it encourages in its ranks. Even the reformist politics represented by Bernie Sanders and the Progressive Caucus are not enough to prevent the depressing trend of US politics the past thirty-five years (at least). Breaking up big banks while keeping a capitalist system in place only means that the banks will get big again. Decrying the police murders of (mostly Black) unarmed citizens will not prevent our militarized police from doing what they are trained to do. Opposing wars without opposing imperialism will only mean there will be more imperial wars. Yet we must do these and more. However, we must also attack the system that creates these abuses.

Our challenge must become broader in its reach and deeper in its analysis. We will then understand that capitalism itself is the problem. So, we must fight capitalism. This is where the "broad in its reach" part comes in. The popularity of the

Sanders campaign and the struggle to raise the minimum wage to fifteen dollars proves that such breadth exists. By deepening the analysis of those campaigns to one that challenges capitalism on its fundamental claim that it is an economic system that works for humanity and making that analysis an essential part of our organizing, it will be possible to involve almost every people in every other social justice struggle, making a broad popular coalition possible. Imagine a movement of groups and individuals dedicated to ending capitalism. If you can't imagine that, at least you can imagine a movement dedicated to insuring free or affordable health care, quality public education and housing for every individual. A movement dedicated to ending the stranglehold of the military-industrial complex and the financial industry on our lives. A movement to end imperial wars. A movement determined to end police brutality and murder. A movement to end systemic racism and make reparations to those so wronged by the racist history of this nation. A movement to end systemic sexism and create gender equality.

If you can imagine such a movement, then you can imagine a movement to end capital-ism—since these are symptoms of that cancer upon humanity's soul. At this point, it seems to be strategically smart to begin with a movement around these reforms, with an approach that encourages an analysis defining capitalism as the root of the problems the movement hopes to reform. Given this, one can certainly see why the movement against Trumpism must not be led by the Democrats, the other capitalist party. Should Democrats participate? Of course. Anyone who opposes Trump and is not a racist or a fascist should participate. However, the ideal goal of any anti-Trumpism movement should be making it considerably more difficult, if not impossible, for the causes of Trumpism to reappear.

> "What is called globalization is really another name for the dominant role of the United States." — Henry Kissinger

There is little essential difference between Trump's idea of US dominance and that represented by the Clinton wing of the Democratic Party. This should be clear by his Cabinet choices alone. The economics of Trump and the Clinton Democrats are variations on the same theme, with very little if any differences between them. Both require overseas investments, minimal regulation on Wall Street, and permanent war. They also require a compliant population in the home country. This is where the popular movement against Trump and Trumpism can play its most vital role. The proto-fascist political agenda he and Congress have planned can be rolled back, but only with a large and protracted movement against it. It will not be an easy task, but it is a necessary one.

Of course, the specific nature of protest movements cannot be planned for in advance. That being said, I cannot repeat enough how paramount it is that the movement against Trumpism should not be led by the Democrats, given the fundamental similarities with the GOP in their understanding of which class should be ruling the USA. The building of a movement is an organic process and in a society as complex as the United States any movement to change that society and the system it maintains will also be complex. In other words, don't expect it to be as simple as the movement that put Trump in power; that movement was never meant to be a genuine protest movement. Indeed, its purpose was and is to further enhance the current system and insure the continued power of the ruling class. This is why the Trump campaign had the support of a very powerful sector of the elites in this country, even if that support was less than enthusiastic from certain quarters. Ultimately, the support from this sector was partly responsible for its current success. It will also be why other elements of the elites currently not on board the Trump train will be on board sooner rather than later. We can already see this taking place as CEOs, some union leaders and politicians from both parties are joined by the media in "normalizing" Trump. The only possible way to prevent Trumpist domination is for a movement to rise against Trumpism and for that movement to become powerful enough to pose a threat to Trumpism and its policies. Only then is there a possibility of a retreat from the drastic rightward turn the rightwing has in mind.

Although we cannot define the specific nature

of any protest movement, we can at least define its politics. We are now in a period when those politics must be radical and anti-capitalist. This means they will also be anti-imperialist. Inside such a definition there exists a politics that is anti-racist and anti-sexist. When one uses the word "radical" it should be understood in terms of its etymology. Merriam-Webster tells us that etymology is this: "Middle English, from Late Latin radicalis, from Latin radic-, radix root…" In other words, it means to go to the root. In politics, this means to find the fundamental cause of the problem one hopes to resolve. In the United States of today, that fundamental cause is capitalism. Hence, any movement against its symptoms, be they in the person of Trump or the Democratic Party, must be a movement against capitalism itself.

This does not mean we should not focus on excesses fostered under Trump. Indeed, if we do not join those protests focused specifically on these issues—racism, sexism, health care, etc.—anti-capitalists will lose a receptive forum and the nation (indeed the world) will suffer the results. There is no room for sectarianism among the anti-capitalist forces. Any break in solidarity will be jumped on by those who oppose us, whether it is Trump and his ilk or the Wall Street wing of the Democratic Party.

Let me quote some lines (with some modifications) from a column I wrote in July 2016, after Trump was crowned as the Republican nominee:

"Of course, the presence of "dark" forces and the threat they represent to Trump and his followers are essential to understanding his appeal. Indeed, the local Gannett broadsheet here in Vermont, introduced Trump's acceptance speech in the next day's paper with this quote from the speech 'safety will be restored....'

It is not the safety of African-American men, whose lives are threatened every time they are confronted by a police officer. It is not the safety of US women and girls, whose lives are threatened by the anti-women policies supported and pushed by Trump's Vice President Mike Pence. It is not the safety of the elderly, who barely get by on a Social Security pension Mr. Trump wants to privatize. It is not the safety of those who can barely pay their bills on minimum wage jobs, when Trump and his staffers have openly questioned the concept of a minimum wage. It is not the safety of immigrants looking for a better life in the United States who Trump wants to round up and deport.

...While Trump pretends that his millennarianist rhetoric will bring the US back to a time my father grew up in—when father knew best and the nation seemed whiter than Ivory Snow soap, (the Democratic Party) promises more of the same corporatist politics in the service of the Goldman-Sachs of the nation.

...In short, we seem to be witnessing a serious split in the US ruling class. Both elements recognize capitalism is in crisis and has been for decades. The two main solutions to this crisis as represented by the campaigns will not solve this crisis, because it is essentially unsolvable. Trump's approach says he can move the capitalist economy back to a time before neoliberalism, when production of goods was almost as important as the financial manipulation of monies for profit and national economies were the primary and dominant macro economy.

It was that manipulation of monies that not only caused the surge in profits for the banking and financial industry. Although this form of speculation has always been part of the capitalist system, it has come to prominence in the last three decades. After the stock market crash of 1929, US financial markets were regulated in order to prevent foreigners from investing too much in national markets and to prevent severe crashes. Some of these rules were modified in the 1980s as a means of bringing more money into the US financial markets. An important change was a loosening of restrictions on foreign investment. Once the rules were loosened, investors from certain oil-rich nations poured money into US markets. These investments, when combined with an aggressive transfer of production facilities to countries in the southern hemisphere and Asia, created a situation that saw US production drop while its income from speculation soared. The following decades have seen further deregulation of the markets, continued transfer of production overseas, and a widening gap between the extremely wealthy and the rest of us. Perhaps one of the most obvious examples of this form of profiteering is the sale of debt packages; where debt (non-existent cash) is packaged and sold, thereby creating a illusion that billions of assets exist where none actually do. If some entity tries to cash this debt in, money has to be produced where there is none—just the promise of it, essentially causing the crash in 2008. This approach was represented best by the Hillary Clinton campaign in 2016. Her approach would (have) continued this trend that Lenin called "the formation of international monopolist capitalist associations which share the world among themselves." This is what the so-called free trade agreements are about. Trump's belief that he can buck this trend runs counter to history, although he seems to think that he is beyond history, except for that which he makes. As I note earlier in this essay, I question Trump's statements in this regard, especially in light of his cabinet choices which seem to indicate that he is more in line with the neoliberal capitalists than he lets on. He is also business partners and friends with current and former executives of Goldman Sachs and financial houses/banks. If one examines Trump's statements (those few he has made regarding this subject), they seem to indicate that he is not against financial speculation, just rules regarding the practice that would limit US dominance of the practice. In other words, his polices would not necessarily discourage speculation like that of the past decades, but would try and make certain that it was US investors that had the advantage. Of course, even this restriction would come up against the way world financial systems operate—a process quite close to that defined by Lenin a century ago.

There is another possibility, too. If Trump tears up the "free trade agreements" of the past thirty years, it creates a scenario where the financial houses can, in essence, make their own rules regarding the manipulation of debt and profit. The only thing preventing a wholesale looting (beyond that currently taking place) would be the US Congress. It is clear to any observer that the Congress is not much interested in preventing any financial institution from profiteering. Indeed, their complicity in the process was essential to creating the current reality.

Neither Trump's fear-ridden America First bluster nor the corporate world order represented by the Democratic Party will prevent war or terrorism. Instead, both will guarantee the continued waste of monies that the permanent war economy is. Trump has called for ending the nuclear agreement with Iran and gone on record calling for an even greater expansion of the US nuclear weapons arsenal. Both the Trump/GOP regime and the Democratic Party also guarantee the continued domination of the US economy by the war industry. Neither representative party of the ruling class has any ideas on how to end the US economy's dependence on the war industry. Nor does it seem either party has any desire to end that dependence.

Neither Donald Trump's administration nor

the Democratic Party leadership represents the people. We should not pretend that they do. To do nothing in these times is not a valid option. Instead, we must get into the streets. This is a struggle that must not waver. This is a struggle that must not fail. Our guiding rationale is simple: when there is a split in the ruling class, it is the task of the Left not to take one side or the other, but to use that split to organize resistance to the system of capitalism itself.

Although our rationale may be simple, our task is not. There will be times when we all want to pack it in and resign ourselves to whatever destiny the rulers have in mind. There will be other times when it will seem the forces arrayed against us are impossible to face, much less defeat. Then there will be times when we win a battle or watch a foe shuffle away in defeat. All of these are part and parcel of any struggle against the rich and powerful. As the abolitionist Frederick Douglass said many decades ago:

> "If there is no struggle, there is no progress. Those who profess to favor freedom, and yet depreciate agitation, are men who want crops without plowing up the ground. They want rain without thunder and lightning. They want the ocean without the awful roar of its many waters. This struggle may be a moral one; or it may be a physical one; or it may be both moral and physical; but it must be a struggle. Power concedes nothing without a demand. It never did and it never will."

We should therefore be ready for anything from lies and slander to brutality. After all, it is when the State and those whom its agents work for are most threatened that state violence becomes the norm. When they are trying to protect what can only be truly termed a criminal enterprise, their tactics will be criminal, too.

Bibliography

Harvey, David. *Rebel Cities: From the Right to the City to the Urban Revolution*. London, New York, Verso. 2013.

Luxemburg, Rosa, Helen Scott, Rosa Luxemburg, and Rosa Luxemburg. *The Essential Rosa Luxemburg: Reform or Revolution & the Mass Strike*. Chicago, Ill: Haymarket Books, 2008.

Marx, Karl, *Capital, A Critique of Political Economy (Das Kapital),* by Karl Marx. Frederick Engels, Ernest Untermann, eds. Samuel Moore, Edward Aveling, trans. 1906.

Smith, John. *Imperialism in the Twenty-First Century: Globalization, Super-Exploitation, and Capitalism's Final Crisis*. New York. Monthly Review Press. 2016

Some of the text is from remarks given to audiences in Olympia, Washington, May 2016.

Made in the USA
Middletown, DE
20 February 2017